STEPHEN ARTERBURN
DAVID STOOP

Tyndale House Publishers, Inc.
Wheaton, Illinois

Visit Tyndale's exciting Web site at
www.tyndale.com

Designed by Timothy R. Botts.

Published in association with the literary
agency of Alive Communications, Inc., 1465
Kelly Johnson Blvd., Suite 320, Colorado
Springs, CO 80920.

Scripture quotations are taken from the *Holy
Bible*, New Living Translation, copyright ©
1996. Used by permission of Tyndale House
Publishers, Inc., Wheaton, Illinois 60189. All
rights reserved.

ISBN 0-8423-6051-4

Printed in the United States of America

06   05   04   03   02   01   00   99   98
10   9   8   7   6   5   4   3   2   1

CONTENTS

MONTH ONE
Allowing God to Help Me Grow As I Submit to His Authority

May your Kingdom come soon. May your will be done here on earth, just as it is in heaven.

MATTHEW 6:10

God is Creator of life and Lord of the universe. But since the Garden of Eden men and women have continually played God and have tried—unsuccessfully—to rule over their own destinies. From Genesis through Revelation, Scripture reveals humankind's natural incapacity to live healthy, God-pleasing lives. The Old Testament describes a colorful assortment of characters who turned their backs on God's ways and inevitably experienced fear, foolishness, and failure. Fortunately, some of them surrendered to the ultimate power of God, allowing him to intervene in their lives with divine power and wisdom. In the New Testament, Christ's death on the cross made God's intervention even more accessible—he took upon himself the willfulness and rebellion of the entire world. His resurrection brought hope for new life.

When we eventually realize that the road we have chosen is not taking us where we need to go, we also understand that to stay on this road is to choose further heartache and destruction. At this point we are willing to admit that our lives have spun out of control and that self-control has failed us. But although we are limited, God is not. By acknowledging that he alone has the power to change the course of our lives and that we are powerless to change it ourselves, we surrender to him and begin the process of spiritual renewal. Only when we relinquish our control to God does he release his supernatural power into our lives; it is only God who can "transform you into a new person by changing the way you think" (Romans 12:2).

Every wound and every weakness is an invitation

to God: "Please do for us what we cannot do for ourselves." When we surrender, we don't just give up or play dead or wait for God to fix us. Surrender is not passivity, nor is it resignation. It is an active and conscious turning toward God through others, reflecting our willingness to submit to his power and to share our truth with others.

Our spiritual renewal is completely dependent upon our reliance on God's power and upon our awareness that we are unable, because of human weaknesses, to live holy or peaceful lives. Only when our human will is relinquished and God's perfect will is submitted to do we receive the help we need to see our lives transformed. True change of heart always begins with the focus on the heart of God.

Life in the Holy Spirit, which brings every aspect of life under the control of God, requires the ultimate surrender of ourselves and complete rest in his grace. It amounts to centering our lives on him, not on ourselves, our dreams, our plans, or our problems.

- Surrender means humbling ourselves before the God of the universe.
- Surrender means admitting that God is all-powerful and releasing our struggles to him.
- Surrender means refusing to escape into the old patterns, habits, and attitudes that continue to distract us from right direction of our lives.
- Surrender means no longer saying, "I can handle this myself."
- Surrender means submitting to God's way of doing things, even though we don't understand it.
- Surrender means getting past our pain and fear and clinging to hope in God and his love for us.
- Surrender means setting aside our human understanding and becoming childlike, acknowledging that we have no answers that work.

THE FIRST KEY FOR SPIRITUAL RENEWAL IS **SURRENDER** TO THE GOD WHO CREATED YOU IN HIS IMAGE.

WEEK ONE *Surrender*

Lord, my heart is not proud; my eyes are not haughty. I don't concern myself with matters too great or awesome for me. But I have stilled and quieted myself, just as a small child is quiet with its mother. Yes, like a small child is my soul within me. Psalm 131:1-2

✳ D A Y 1   12/29/98

The Lord took me to :— Is 14: 24-32
the Lord has cast satan down + Gods
purposes will prevail. Vs 25:b his yoke shall
depart from them, + his burden from their
shoulder. Vs 27 For the Lord of hosts has purposed +
who will annul it? His hand is stretched out, who will turn it back.

✳ D A Y 2

_____

_____

_____

_____

_____

✳ D A Y 3

_____

_____

_____

_____

_____

✳ D A Y 4

_____

_____

_____

_____

✳ D A Y 5

_____

_____

_____

_____

PRAYER REQUESTS

_____

_____

_____

GOD'S RESPONSE AND MY THOUGHTS

_____

_____

_____

Have Thine own way, Lord! Have Thine own way!
Thou art the potter; I am the clay.
Mold me and make me after Thy will,
While I am waiting, yielded and still.
Adelaide Addison Pollard

WEEK TWO *Surrender*

I know the one in whom I trust, and I am sure that he is able to guard what I have entrusted to him until the day of his return. 2 Timothy 1:12

✳ D A Y   1

_____

_____

_____

_____

_____

✳ D A Y   2

_____

_____

_____

_____

_____

✳ D A Y   3

_____

_____

_____

_____

_____

✳ D A Y 4

_____

_____

_____

_____

✳ D A Y 5

_____

_____

_____

_____

PRAYER REQUESTS

_____

_____

_____

GOD'S RESPONSE AND MY THOUGHTS

_____

_____

_____

Do with me whatever it shall please thee. For it can not be anything but good, whatever thou shalt do with me. If it be thy will I should be in darkness, be thou blessed; and if it be thy will I should be in light, be thou again blessed. If thou grant me comfort, be thou blessed; and if thou wilt have me afflicted, be thou still equally blessed. My son, such as this ought to be thy state, if thou desire to walk with me. Thou must be as ready to suffer as to rejoice. Thou must cheerfully be as destitute and poor, as full and rich.
Thomas à Kempis

WEEK THREE *Surrender*

*So humble yourselves under the mighty power of God,
and in his good time he will honor you.* 1 Peter 5:6

✳ D A Y 1

_____

_____

_____

_____

_____

✳ D A Y 2

_____

_____

_____

_____

_____

✳ D A Y 3

_____

_____

_____

_____

_____

✽ D A Y 4

_____

_____

_____

_____

_____

✽ D A Y 5

_____

_____

_____

_____

_____

PRAYER REQUESTS

_____

_____

_____

GOD'S RESPONSE AND MY THOUGHTS

_____

_____

_____

Few souls understand what God would accomplish in them if they were to abandon themselves unreservedly to Him and if they were to allow His grace to mold them accordingly.
Ignatius of Loyola

WEEK FOUR *Surrender*

O Israel, how can you say the Lord does not see your troubles? How can you say God refuses to hear your case? Have you never heard or understood? Don't you know that the Lord is the everlasting God, the Creator of all the earth? He never grows faint or weary. No one can measure the depths of his understanding. He gives power to those who are tired and worn out; he offers strength to the weak. Isaiah 40:27-29

✳ D A Y 1

_____

_____

_____

_____

_____

✳ D A Y 2

_____

_____

_____

_____

_____

✳ D A Y 3

_____

_____

_____

_____

_____

✲ DAY 4

✲ DAY 5

PRAYER REQUESTS

GOD'S RESPONSE AND MY THOUGHTS

And since He bids me seek His face,
Believe His Word, and trust His grace,
I'll cast on Him my every care
And wait for thee, sweet hour of prayer!
William W. Walford

MONTH TWO
Accepting the Full Reality of My Situation

O Lord, you have examined my heart and know everything about me.

PSALM 139:1

As we begin to acknowledge the grim futility of our existence and the abandonment of God's ways that led to it, our eyes begin to open. We see that our lives are dangerously at risk. Through self-examination, we confront our sins, character defects, habits, and areas of irresponsibility, becoming aware that unless we change our course, we may be headed toward physical, emotional, and spiritual disaster.

All of us struggle with blind spots in our lives, and to some degree we all live in denial and self-deception. Rather than see our areas of sin and pain, we tend to point to others and focus on them, or we find ways to distract or anesthetize ourselves. God wants us to look at the big lie of our lives, realizing that the road we're on is actually a detour we have taken to avoid facing our own hurts and failures. That detour can involve many things that keep us from growing spiritually. Breaking through denial means becoming aware of our sin and our pain and consciously confronting the sick behaviors and patterns that have detoured us.

Once, with God's help, we remove our blinders, deception and denial are brought to an end and we begin to see ourselves as we really are: trapped in our sins, paralyzed by fear, and doing things that produce short-term results rather than long-term change. We also come to see God as he is: patient, loving, and "able to accomplish infinitely more than we would ever dare to ask or hope" (Ephesians 3:20).

By facing ourselves honestly, we are moved out of the past and into the reality of the present. Here,

God can teach us to resolve our problems rather than reproduce them in family and close friends.

Seeing the reality of my situation helps me focus on what I can do to change rather than on what I want others to do to make me feel better. It means becoming humble enough to confront who I really am, what my motives truly are, and what actually causes the conflicts I experience.

Finding and facing reality requires the help of God. If we ask for help in seeing, we can trust him to provide it. It will probably come from others, who are kind enough to speak the truth in love, particularly when we humble ourselves and ask for help. Help will also come through our own prayer, reflection, and daily experience. We can be sure of this—God wants to teach us to face up to the truth about our lives.

- ◆ To See It means we stop lying to ourselves about the failures, sins, and heartaches in our lives and begin to acknowledge the truth about our situation.
- ◆ To See It means we consider the fact that what we criticize in others is often a clue to what we may be denying in ourselves.
- ◆ To See It means we face our past, our pain, and our failures head-on.
- ◆ To See It means we sift through the issues of our lives.
- ◆ To See It means we seek, receive, and apply God's wisdom.
- ◆ To See It means we stop distracting ourselves with activities, substances, or other diversions and face the realities in which we live.
- ◆ To See It means we look at what we've done and where we are in light of God's mercy and grace.
- ◆ To See It means we accept that we are unable to help ourselves without God's intervention and assistance.

THE SECOND KEY FOR SPIRITUAL RENEWAL IS TO **SEE** THE REALITY OF WHO YOU ARE AND THE CHALLENGES YOU FACE.

WEEK ONE *See It*

Search me, O God, and know my heart; test me and know my thoughts. Point out anything in me that offends you, and lead me along the path of everlasting life. Psalm 139:23-24

✲ DAY 1

✲ DAY 2

✲ DAY 3

✻ D A Y 4

_____

_____

_____

_____

_____

✻ D A Y 5

_____

_____

_____

_____

PRAYER REQUESTS

_____

_____

_____

GOD'S RESPONSE AND MY THOUGHTS

_____

_____

_____

*Let us test and examine our ways. Let us turn again
in repentance to the Lord.*
Lamentations 3:40

WEEK TWO *See It*

I will lead blind Israel down a new path, guiding them along an unfamiliar way. I will make the darkness bright before them and smooth out the road ahead of them. Yes, I will indeed do these things; I will not forsake them. Isaiah 42:16

✳ D A Y 1

_____

_____

_____

_____

_____

✳ D A Y 2

_____

_____

_____

_____

_____

✳ D A Y 3

_____

_____

_____

_____

_____

✳ D A Y   4

_____

_____

_____

_____

_____

✳ D A Y   5

_____

_____

_____

_____

PRAYER REQUESTS

_____

_____

_____

GOD'S RESPONSE AND MY THOUGHTS

_____

_____

_____

*It happens . . . that most of the proud never really
    discover their true selves.
They think they have conquered their passions
and they find out how poor they really are only after
    they die.*
Climacus

WEEK THREE *See It*

Each time he said, "My gracious favor is all you need. My power works best in your weakness." So now I am glad to boast about my weaknesses, so that the power of Christ may work through me. Since I know it is all for Christ's good, I am quite content with my weaknesses and with insults, hardships, persecutions, and calamities. For when I am weak, then I am strong. 2 Corinthians 12:9-10

✳ D A Y 1

_____

_____

_____

_____

_____

✳ D A Y 2

_____

_____

_____

_____

_____

✳ D A Y 3

_____

_____

_____

_____

_____

✲ DAY 4

✲ DAY 5

PRAYER REQUESTS

GOD'S RESPONSE AND MY THOUGHTS

Out of my bondage, sorrow and night, Jesus, I come,
Jesus, I come;
Into Thy freedom, gladness and light, Jesus, I come
to Thee.
William T. Sleeper

WEEK FOUR *See It*

O Lord, you have examined my heart and know everything about me. You know when I sit down or stand up. You know my every thought when far away. You chart the path ahead of me and tell me where to stop and rest. Every moment you know where I am. You know what I am going to say even before I say it, Lord. Psalm 139:1-4

✲ DAY 1

✲ DAY 2

✲ DAY 3

✳ D A Y 4

_____

_____

_____

_____

_____

✳ D A Y 5

_____

_____

_____

_____

_____

PRAYER REQUESTS

_____

_____

_____

GOD'S RESPONSE AND MY THOUGHTS

_____

_____

_____

Do you need to reach out to someone or some people to discover the areas of your life that need work? Are you blind to what others see? If so, ask for help.

Reach out to others and allow them to reach into your world and help you see who you are—the wonders and the blunders. If you can see the reality, then and only then can you hope to change it.

MONTH THREE
Beginning to Open Up about the Reality of My Life

Confess your sins to each other and pray for each other so that you may be healed.

JAMES 5:16

There is sickness in secrecy. The sinning psalmist said, "When I refused to confess my sin, I was weak and miserable, and I groaned all day long." When we are willing to be open, healing becomes possible. By breaking our silence and speaking the truth about ourselves aloud to another person, we move out of the darkness and bring our secrets into the light. Confessing our sins and talking about the sins done to us are other keys to spiritual healing and health.

It is clearly important to God that men and women verbally express the struggles that are hidden in their hearts. Verbalization gives substance to inarticulate thoughts, and words affirm the realities of which we have become aware. Even on the key issue of Christian salvation, belief is to be affirmed with spoken words. Paul wrote, "If you confess with your mouth that Jesus is Lord and believe in your heart that God raised him from the dead, you will be saved. For it is by believing in your heart that you are made right with God, and it is by confessing with your mouth that you are saved" (Romans 10:9-10).

In similar terms, when we confess our sins, the words we speak give a concrete dimension to subtle compromises and behaviors that might otherwise remain unclear in our minds. By telling others of sins and shortcomings in our lives, we confirm our awareness of those faults and we become obedient to God's ways of working in the lives of his children. Unexpressed thoughts are exempt from the input of other Christians, who can both challenge and help us to see the truth. When we confess our faults, we put others in the position of advising us, praying for us, and sharing our struggles. In openness we humble ourselves before others.

Confession requires openness, and openness requires vulnerability. Confession also requires confidentiality. Confession is an invitation to intimacy, and it involves trust in both God and another person—a trust that is necessary if we are to fully reveal our secrets. Unless we open ourselves, whatever help we receive from others will not thoroughly address our real needs and conflicts. Openness is an outward act of trust that enables us to cleanse our souls from the inside out. To Say It means we submit ourselves to God's way of handling secrets, respecting his desire for openness and vulnerability among his people.

When we verbally express our needs, weaknesses, and failures to another person, we affirm our intentions toward health, healing, and a new life. When we verbally confess our sins to God, we acknowledge his holiness and our unworthiness. Through confession, we invite him to cleanse us and to free us from our guilt and shame so we can move forward with him in uninterrupted relationship.

◆ To Say It means we are willing to overcome our fear of rejection by revealing our failures to another person.
◆ To Say It means we reject our habit of self-protective secretiveness.
◆ To Say It means we admit to at least one other person that we have fallen short of God's best.
◆ To Say It means we have stopped trying to hide our true feelings.
◆ To Say It means we have chosen to humble ourselves before God and other people.
◆ To Say It means we renounce our independence and admit that we need help from fellow believers.
◆ To Say It means we put our vague sense of guilt into written or spoken words and express the situation without making excuses.

THE THIRD KEY FOR SPIRITUAL RENEWAL IS TO **SAY** TO ANOTHER WHAT I KNOW TO BE TRUE ABOUT MYSELF.

WEEK ONE *Say It*

When I refused to confess my sin, I was weak and miserable, and I groaned all day long. Day and night your hand of discipline was heavy on me. My strength evaporated like water in the summer heat. Finally, I confessed all my sins to you and stopped trying to hide them. I said to myself, "I will confess my rebellion to the Lord." And you forgave me! All my guilt is gone. Psalm 32:3-5

✻ D A Y 1

_____

_____

_____

_____

_____

✻ D A Y 2

_____

_____

_____

_____

_____

✻ D A Y 3

_____

_____

_____

_____

_____

✳ D A Y 4

_____

_____

_____

_____

_____

✳ D A Y 5

_____

_____

_____

_____

_____

PRAYER REQUESTS

_____

_____

_____

GOD'S RESPONSE AND MY THOUGHTS

_____

_____

_____

Confess yourself to heaven;
Repent what's past;
Avoid what is to come.
William Shakespeare *(Hamlet)*

WEEK TWO *Say It*

If we say we have no sin, we are only fooling ourselves and refusing to accept the truth. But if we confess our sins to him, he is faithful and just to forgive us and to cleanse us from every wrong. 1 John 1:8-9

✻ D A Y 1

_____

_____

_____

_____

_____

✻ D A Y 2

_____

_____

_____

_____

_____

✻ D A Y 3

_____

_____

_____

_____

_____

�֍ D A Y 4

_____

_____

_____

_____

_____

�֍ D A Y 5

_____

_____

_____

_____

_____

PRAYER REQUESTS

_____

_____

_____

GOD'S RESPONSE AND MY THOUGHTS

_____

_____

_____

When Christ's faithful strive to confess all the sins that they can remember, they undoubtedly place all of them before the divine mercy for pardon. But those who fail to do so and knowingly withhold some, place nothing before the divine goodness for remission . . . for if the sick person is too ashamed to show his wound to the doctor, the medicine cannot heal what it does not know.
Council of Trent, 1551

WEEK THREE *Say It*

People who cover over their sins will not prosper. But if they confess and forsake them, they will receive mercy. Blessed are those who have a tender conscience, but the stubborn are headed for serious trouble.
Proverbs 28:13-14

✲ DAY 1

✲ DAY 2

✲ DAY 3

✳ D A Y 4

_____

_____

_____

_____

_____

✳ D A Y 5

_____

_____

_____

_____

_____

PRAYER REQUESTS

_____

_____

_____

GOD'S RESPONSE AND MY THOUGHTS

_____

_____

_____

Almighty and most merciful Father, we have erred, and strayed from Thy ways like lost sheep. We have offended against Thy holy laws. We have left undone those things which we ought to have done, and we have done those things which we ought not to have done; and there is no health in us.
The General Confession, *Book of Common Prayer*

Kyrie Eleison.
Jesus Christ, Lamb of God, Savior, Have mercy on me.
The Mass

WEEK FOUR *Say It*

The next day John saw Jesus coming toward him and said, "Look! There is the Lamb of God who takes away the sin of the world!" John 1:29

✳ D A Y 1

_____

_____

_____

_____

_____

✳ D A Y 2

_____

_____

_____

_____

_____

✳ D A Y 3

_____

_____

_____

_____

_____

✻ D A Y   4

_____

_____

_____

_____

_____

✻ D A Y   5

_____

_____

_____

_____

_____

PRAYER REQUESTS

_____

_____

_____

GOD'S RESPONSE AND MY THOUGHTS

_____

_____

_____

Can we find a friend so faithful
Who will all our sorrows share?
Jesus knows our every weakness,
Take it to the Lord in prayer.
Joseph Medlicott Scriven

MONTH FOUR
Accepting Responsibility to Make the Changes That Must Be Made for Spiritual Growth to Occur

We are each responsible for our own conduct.

GALATIANS 6:5

Taking responsibility for our problems entails two realities: experience and ownership. In many instances, the hurts that have driven us into inappropriate behaviors—destructive habits—are hurts that we have never fully worked through. Although it requires God-given courage to walk through our pain and to grieve our losses, the process of doing so is an indispensable element in our healing.

The avoidance of pain and problems is a natural human response. Most people feel they have suffered enough and have no desire to feel overwhelmed by sorrowful emotions. But grief is a necessary process in a fallen world, and grief over our failures and losses will connect us to God's grace. St. Augustine affirmed this, saying, "In my deepest wound I saw your glory and it dazzled me." No one has experienced as much pain as Jesus did as he agonized in the garden and shed his blood on the cross.

How easy it is to blame others around us for everything that has gone wrong. Accepting responsibility is a bold step in which we take the reality of our lives and allow God to use it to change us: He shapes us into his character as we follow his ways. This part of the process will bring us face-to-face with our pain and loss—not a pleasant experience. But by confronting these, with God's help, we are able to press on into the new life he has planned for us.

Rather than continue in patterns of self-pity and paralysis, at this point we courageously pick up the pieces of our lives, and with God's help we take full responsibility as we deal with our challenges.

- To Own It means we face our problems rather than escape them.
- To Own It means we take the time to bury our losses and grieve them.
- To Own It means we believe Jesus' words: "God blesses those who mourn, for they will be comforted" (Matthew 5:4).
- To Own It means we stop playing the role of victim.
- To Own It means we are willing to bear the full responsibility of our misconduct.
- To Own It means we no longer blame others for our sins.
- To Own It means that we reach out to Christ, who is fully capable of understanding our emotional pain, having suffered abuse and rejection himself.
- To Own It means we look beyond our losses at God's deeper purposes.
- To Own It means we accept the hope that God's plans for us are always good and loving.

THE FOURTH KEY FOR SPIRITUAL RENEWAL IS TO **OWN** MY SITUATION, TO ACCEPT FULL RESPONSIBILITY FOR MY PART IN IT, AND TO SEEK GOD'S HELP IN MAKING ANY NECESSARY CHANGES.

WEEK ONE *Own it*

In times of trouble, may the Lord respond to your cry.
May the God of Israel keep you safe from all harm.
                                        Psalm 20:1

✳ D A Y 1

_____

_____

_____

_____

✳ D A Y 2

_____

_____

_____

_____

✳ D A Y 3

_____

_____

_____

_____

✳ D A Y 4

_____

_____

_____

_____

_____

_____

_____

_____

_____

PRAYER REQUESTS

_____

_____

_____

GOD'S RESPONSE AND MY THOUGHTS

_____

_____

_____

There are several possible sources for the pain in our lives:

- Natural complications such as birth defects and diseases, and tragedies such as hurricanes, fires, and floods
- Inadvertent wrongs done to us by others for which blame cannot be applied
- Wrongs done to us by others for which they must be held responsible
- Wrongs we do to ourselves; sometimes this involves our refusal to confront inappropriate behavior in others, thus allowing them to hurt us

Authentic faith acknowledges God's right to allow certain things to happen in our lives, whether we "deserve" them or not. Faith also requires us to deal with our difficulties in a humble and godly manner.

WEEK TWO *Own It*

*Let me hear of your unfailing love to me in the morning,
for I am trusting you. Show me where to walk, for I have
come to you in prayer.* Psalm 143:8

✳ D A Y 1

✳ D A Y 2

✳ D A Y 3

✳ D A Y 4

✳ D A Y 5

PRAYER REQUESTS

GOD'S RESPONSE AND MY THOUGHTS

Not a shadow can rise, not a cloud in the skies,
But His smile quickly drives it away;
Not a doubt nor a fear, not a sigh nor a tear,
Can abide while we trust and obey.
John H. Sammis

WEEK THREE *Own it*

As you endure this divine discipline, remember that God is treating you as his own children. . . . So take a new grip with your tired hands and stand firm on your shaky legs. Hebrews 12:7, 12

✳ D A Y 1

_____

_____

_____

_____

_____

✳ D A Y 2

_____

_____

_____

_____

_____

✳ D A Y 3

_____

_____

_____

_____

_____

_____

_____

_____

_____

_____

✻ D A Y 5

_____

_____

_____

_____

_____

PRAYER REQUESTS

_____

_____

_____

GOD'S RESPONSE AND MY THOUGHTS

_____

_____

_____

In me there is darkness,
But with Thee there is light.
I am lonely, but Thou leavest me not.
I am feeble in heart, but Thou leavest me not.
I am restless, but with Thee there is peace.
In me there is bitterness, but with Thee there is patience;
Thy ways are past understanding,
But Thou knowest the way for me.
Dietrich Bonhoeffer

WEEK FOUR *Own It*

The steps of the godly are directed by the Lord. He delights in every detail of their lives. Though they stumble, they will not fall, for the Lord holds them by the hand. Psalm 37:23-24

✻ D A Y   1

_____

_____

_____

_____

_____

✻ D A Y   2

_____

_____

_____

_____

_____

✻ D A Y   3

_____

_____

_____

_____

_____

✳ D A Y 4

_____

_____

_____

_____

✳ D A Y 5

_____

_____

_____

_____

PRAYER REQUESTS

_____

_____

_____

GOD'S RESPONSE AND MY THOUGHTS

_____

_____

_____

*I asked God for strength, that I might achieve; I was
   made weak, that I might learn humbly to obey.*
*I asked for health, that I might do greater things; I was
   given infirmity, that I might do better things.*
*I asked for riches, that I might be happy; I was given
   poverty, that I might be wise.*
*I got nothing that I asked for—but everything I had
   hoped for;*
*Almost despite myself, my unspoken prayers were
   answered.*
I am among all men most richly blessed.
Unknown

MONTH FIVE
Forgiving My Own Failures and the Failures of Those Who Have Hurt Me

If you forgive those who sin against you, your heavenly Father will forgive you. But if you refuse to forgive others, your Father will not forgive your sins.

MATTHEW 6:14-15

Forgiving and receiving forgiveness are gracious acts of love. These acts have supernatural power to change both the life of the forgiven and the one who forgives. When we look at all for which God has forgiven us, it moves us to find a way to forgive others even if they have hurt us deeply. The Cross of Christ allows this in a dimension far beyond our own power to forgive.

Forgiveness is inextricably woven into Christian salvation. Jesus clearly taught that unless we forgive others, we cannot be forgiven by our heavenly Father. At first glance, this may appear to be a rigid and rigorous principle, but it is God's means of extending his grace to everyone. When we refuse to forgive, we play "God" in the lives of others and pass our judgment on them. This interferes with the process of grace Jesus Christ initiated at the cross.

Forgiveness can be difficult—almost impossible—for those who have been severely abused physically, sexually, and even spiritually. It is never easy or instant, and it may take years to complete. However, if forgiveness isn't rendered, it is the injured person who remains trapped in the abuse of the past. Not to forgive allows others to continue to abuse us as we endlessly relive their offenses. Our yesterdays must be put in the past so we can fully enjoy today.

The forgiveness process also involves making things right with those we have wounded. This may require us to write letters or make phone calls, to repay debts, to make amends or otherwise do our part in making wrongs as right as possible. This, of course, can result in enormous spiritual blessings, both to others and to us.

Forgiveness, when empowered by God's Spirit, is a process of detaching painful events from our emotional response to them, thus facilitating the process of healing. In contrast, the refusal to forgive has far-reaching results spiritually, emotionally, and even physically.

Forgiving and accepting forgiveness release us from the past. The history of our lives cannot be changed, but forgiveness sets us free from the emotional turmoil those past hurts, betrayals, and abuses have caused. Forgiveness, of course, does not condone or excuse others' misbehavior. It does, however, prevent us from being repeatedly abused and controlled by the abuser.

◆ To Release It means we hand back our rights to God (the rights we have snatched from him) and invite him to be in charge.
◆ To Release It means we ask for forgiveness and make restitution for the damage we've done.
◆ To Release It means we no longer energize ourselves with rage or hatred.
◆ To Release It means we stop trying to change other people and ask God to do it.
◆ To Release It means we step out of the past and into the present.
◆ To Release It means we accept the pardon of the Cross for others as well as for ourselves.
◆ To Release It means we obey Jesus' instructions to forgive so that we can be forgiven.
◆ To Release It means we begin a process of forgiveness that may continue for a lifetime.
◆ To Release It means we live in the light of God's forgiveness.

THE FIFTH KEY FOR SPIRITUAL RENEWAL IS TO **RELEASE** OUR PAST SO THAT IT DOES NOT IMPEDE OUR FUTURE.

WEEK ONE *Release It*

Be kind to each other, tenderhearted, forgiving one another, just as God through Christ has forgiven you.
Ephesians 4:32

✲ DAY 1

✲ DAY 2

✲ DAY 3

✻ D A Y 4

_____

_____

_____

_____

_____

✻ D A Y 5

_____

_____

_____

_____

_____

PRAYER REQUESTS

_____

_____

_____

GOD'S RESPONSE AND MY THOUGHTS

_____

_____

_____

Savior, Thy dying love Thou gavest me,
Nothing should I withhold, Dear Lord, from Thee.
S. D. Phelps

WEEK TWO *Release It*

"Shouldn't you have mercy on your fellow servant, just as I had mercy on you?" Then the angry king sent the man to prison until he had paid every penny. That's what my heavenly Father will do to you if you refuse to forgive your brothers and sisters in your heart.
Matthew 18:33-35

✳ D A Y 1

_____

_____

_____

_____

_____

✳ D A Y 2

_____

_____

_____

_____

_____

✳ D A Y 3

_____

_____

_____

_____

_____

✳ D A Y 4

_____
_____
_____
_____
_____

✳ D A Y 5

_____
_____
_____
_____
_____

PRAYER REQUESTS

_____
_____
_____

GOD'S RESPONSE AND MY THOUGHTS

_____
_____
_____

*If you forgive and forget in the usual sense, you're just
driving what you remember into the subconscious; it
stays there and festers. But to look upon what you
remember and know you've forgiven is achievement.*
Faith Baldwin

WEEK THREE *Release It*

You must make allowance for each other's faults and forgive the person who offends you. Remember, the Lord forgave you, so you must forgive others. And the most important piece of clothing you must wear is love. Love is what binds us all together in perfect harmony.
Colossians 3:13-14

✲ DAY 1

✲ DAY 2

✲ DAY 3

✽ D A Y 4

_____

_____

_____

_____

✽ D A Y 5

_____

_____

_____

_____

PRAYER REQUESTS

_____

_____

_____

GOD'S RESPONSE AND MY THOUGHTS

_____

_____

_____

Blest be the tie that binds our hearts in Christian love:
The fellowship of kindred minds is like to that above.

Before our Father's throne we pour our ardent prayers;
Our fears, our hopes, our aims are one, our comforts and
*   our cares.*

We share each other's woes, our mutual burdens bear,
And often for each other flows the sympathizing tear.

When we asunder part, it gives us inward pain;
But we shall still be joined in heart, and hope to meet
*   again.*
John Fawcett

WEEK FOUR *Release It*

Then Peter came to him and asked, "Lord, how often should I forgive someone who sins against me? Seven times?" "No!" Jesus replied, "seventy times seven!"
Matthew 18:21-22

✳ D A Y   1

✳ D A Y   2

✳ D A Y   3

✻ DAY 4

_____

_____

_____

_____

_____

✻ DAY 5

_____

_____

_____

_____

_____

PRAYER REQUESTS

_____

_____

_____

GOD'S RESPONSE AND MY THOUGHTS

_____

_____

_____

Reconciliation with God leads, as it were, to other reconciliations, which repair the other breaches caused by sin.
John Paul II

MONTH SIX
Transforming My Pain into a Purposeful Ministry out of My Desire to Share with Others

All praise to the God and Father of our Lord Jesus Christ. He is the source of every mercy and the God who comforts us. He comforts us in all our troubles so that we can comfort others. When others are troubled, we will be able to give them the same comfort God has given us.

2 CORINTHIANS 1:3-4

We can never know God's plans or his gain from our loss, unless we give him our misery and allow him to transform it into a mission for our lives. Once our loss and pain point us to God's grace, we can also lead others into it. In doing so, we partner with God as he accomplishes his purposes. After we emerge from our own despair, become transparent, and candidly share our victories, we will be in a position to share our struggles and God's power to overcome, attracting others into his grace.

The Christian gospel brings a profound message about earthly evil being transformed into eternal good: Weakness into strength, tragedy into triumph, loss into gain, mortality into immortality, death into life. These concepts might be superficially discounted as theological abstractions, except that they translate into inescapable day-by-day miracles that are clearly evident in the lives of Christian believers throughout the world.

The cosmic turning point in the transformation of evil to good is the death and resurrection of Jesus Christ. We activate this process in our personal lives through faith in God's Son, through hope in his good and loving character, and through relinquishment of our lives to his flawless will.

Once we have surrendered ourselves to the power and love of God, we become aware of the profound changes and new avenues of hope he has created in our lives. And once we have forgiven others, our most difficult experiences leave us with a greater capacity for empathy and compassion. Our ability to love has deepened. We have become more honest. Our hearts are full of gratitude. Living in the grace God has given us, becoming aware of the gifts of the Spirit, and feeling the joy of spiritual renewal, we are compelled to carry the wonderful message of spiritual transformation to others. We reverse and defuse our own heartaches and losses by reaching out to those facing similar struggles. Unless we give away our miracle to others, we stifle God's message and miss out on God's blessings for us.

- ◆ To Redeem It means to participate in God's process of working all things together for good.
- ◆ To Redeem It means to step out of our own pain and into the needs of others.
- ◆ To Redeem It means to seek ways of applying past pain to positive purposes.
- ◆ To Redeem It means we stop saying, "Why me, Lord?" and start saying, "What do you want me to do?"
- ◆ To Redeem It means being a giver instead of a taker.
- ◆ To Redeem It means learning to listen rather than always needing to be heard.
- ◆ To Redeem It means we allow our humbling experiences to give us a servant's heart.
- ◆ To Redeem It means investing our spiritual gifts in the lives of others.

THE SIXTH
KEY TO
SPIRITUAL
RENEWAL
IS TO ALLOW
GOD TO
**REDEEM AND
TRANSFORM**
ALL THAT I AM
AND ALL I HAVE
BEEN THROUGH
INTO A
PURPOSEFUL
MINISTRY
OF LOVE FOR
OTHERS.

WEEK ONE *Redeem It*

Now glory be to God! By his mighty power at work within us, he is able to accomplish infinitely more than we would ever dare to ask or hope. Ephesians 3:20

✽ D A Y 1

_____

_____

_____

_____

_____

✽ D A Y 2

_____

_____

_____

_____

_____

✽ D A Y 3

_____

_____

_____

_____

_____

✳ D A Y 4

_____

_____

_____

_____

_____

✳ D A Y 5

_____

_____

_____

_____

_____

PRAYER REQUESTS

_____

_____

_____

GOD'S RESPONSE AND MY THOUGHTS

_____

_____

_____

This is the real purpose of our pain—to put us in touch with Jesus.

Pain gives us the privilege of walking in his footsteps.

It is a necessary journey, this trek through the valley of the shadow of death.

It is part of our calling as Christians.

We are intended not only to experience the gloom of loss but also to rejoice in the ultimate glory of resurrection.

WEEK TWO *Redeem It*

And we know that God causes everything to work together for the good of those who love God and are called according to his purpose for them. Romans 8:28

✳ D A Y   1

_____

_____

_____

_____

_____

✳ D A Y   2

_____

_____

_____

_____

_____

✳ D A Y   3

_____

_____

_____

_____

_____

✻ DAY 4

_____

_____

_____

_____

_____

✻ DAY 5

_____

_____

_____

_____

PRAYER REQUESTS

_____

_____

_____

GOD'S RESPONSE AND MY THOUGHTS

_____

_____

_____

A reporter once asked the great inventor Thomas Edison, "How does it feel to have failed so many times in one pursuit?" Edison was adamant in his answer: "I have not failed ten thousand times. I have successfully found ten thousand ways that will not work."

WEEK THREE *Redeem It*

*All praise to the God and Father of our Lord Jesus
Christ. He is the source of every mercy and the God who
comforts us. He comforts us in all our troubles so that we
can comfort others. When others are troubled, we will be
able to give them the same comfort God has given us.
You can be sure that the more we suffer for Christ, the
more God will shower us with his comfort through
Christ. So when we are weighed down with troubles, it is
for your benefit and salvation! For when God comforts
us, it is so that we, in turn, can be an encouragement to
you. Then you can patiently endure the same things we
suffer. We are confident that as you share in suffering,
you will also share God's comfort.* 2 Corinthians 1:3-7

✳ D A Y   1

✳ D A Y   2

✳ D A Y   3

✳ D A Y 4

_____

_____

_____

_____

_____

✳ D A Y 5

_____

_____

_____

_____

_____

PRAYER REQUESTS

_____

_____

_____

GOD'S RESPONSE AND MY THOUGHTS

_____

_____

_____

When we are transformed by the power of God, our problems are transformed also. What caused our pain becomes an ointment for the pain of others. Our wandering in darkness becomes a beacon of illuminating hope as we turn our problems into a platform to reach others. God transforms us, and we transform all that we have been through into a new mission with purpose and meaning. Love makes it the natural thing to do.

WEEK FOUR *Redeem It*

The Spirit of the Sovereign Lord is upon me, because the Lord has appointed me to bring good news to the poor. He has sent me to comfort the brokenhearted and to announce that captives will be released and prisoners will be freed. He has sent me to tell those who mourn that the time of the Lord's favor has come, and with it, the day of God's anger against their enemies. To all who mourn in Israel, he will give beauty for ashes, joy instead of mourning, praise instead of despair. For the Lord has planted them like strong and graceful oaks for his own glory. Isaiah 61:1-3

✳ D A Y   1

_____

_____

_____

_____

✳ D A Y   2

_____

_____

_____

_____

✳ D A Y   3

_____

_____

_____

_____

�֍ D A Y 4

_____ _____

_____

_____

_____

_____

�֍ D A Y 5

_____

_____

_____

_____

_____

PRAYER REQUESTS

_____

_____

_____

GOD'S RESPONSE AND MY THOUGHTS

_____

_____

_____

The gifts we read about in the New Testament
include the following:

Serving ◆ Helping ◆ Mercy ◆ Hospitality
Tongues ◆ Healing ◆ Exhortation ◆ Giving
Wisdom ◆ Knowledge ◆ Faith ◆ Apostleship/Ministry
Evangelism ◆ Prophecy ◆ Teaching ◆ Pastoring
Leadership ◆ Administration ◆ Miracles
Interpretation of Tongues

Protecting the Spiritual Gains I Have Made and Persevering through Life's Inevitable Struggles

So make every effort to apply the benefits of these promises to your life. Then your faith will produce a life of moral excellence. A life of moral excellence leads to knowing God better.

2 PETER 1:5

Surrendering to God's love and authority is a life-long endeavor. And by the time we have made our way through the process of spiritual transformation, we know that we need other Christians to help us stay on the right path. Without them, we are likely to return to patterns of secrecy, sin, and sickness.

When we place ourselves in a position of accountability to others, we invite their scrutiny. At first this goes against our natural bent and seems like an invasion of our privacy. But accountability to others is an invaluable means of preventing a recurrence of our sinful behavior. The removal of secrets from our lives was essential to our healing; now we need to introduce spiritual disciplines into our lives so that we are not entrapped by either overconfidence or a return to secret sins.

Paul wrote, "We should be decent and true in everything we do, so that everyone can approve of our behavior. . . . Let the Lord Jesus Christ take control of you, and don't think of ways to indulge your evil desires" (Romans 13:13-14). We are able to remain decent and true only because God is with us, upholding us and giving us new life. By continually surrendering to his will, and through ongoing and honest accountability to trustworthy individuals, we are able to take the message of renewal and transformation to other hurting people, never forgetting where we came from and how we got where we are.

Scripture indicates that human willfulness is at odds with God's plan for his people. He created us to be entirely dependent upon him, continuing to repent of our sins and to return to his ways. He wants us to communicate with him in prayer. He has also indicated, in his description of the multi-dimensional body of Christ (1 Corinthians 12, Romans 12), that we are meant to be dependent upon other Christians. Our sinful human nature has always given us the message that we can handle life quite well on our own. However, God's Word and painful experiences remind us that we can't.

Through accountability and through the practice of spiritual disciplines, we continue to move forward into our new lives, practicing our surrender to God on a daily basis. In so doing, we prevent ourselves from slipping back into old destructive relationships and situations.

♦ To Preserve It means we establish boundaries that prevent our return to sick and sinful behavior.
♦ To Preserve It means we continue to forgive and to be forgiven.
♦ To Preserve It means we avoid secrecy by remaining accountable to others, while also being a trustworthy confidant for their secrets.
♦ To Preserve It means we choose to be part of a godly community.
♦ To Preserve It means reading God's Word, meditating upon it, and praying daily.
♦ To Preserve It means developing, with God's help, a deep and godly character.
♦ To Preserve It means being patient with ourselves when we slip.
♦ To Preserve It means moving forward while remembering where we've been.
♦ To Preserve It means continuing the process of surrender—day by day, year by year.

THE SEVENTH KEY FOR SPIRITUAL RENEWAL IS TO **PRESERVE** THE SPIRITUAL GROUND WE HAVE GAINED THROUGH THE POWER OF GOD.

WEEK ONE *Preserve It*

*Dear brothers and sisters, you are foreigners and aliens
here. So I warn you to keep away from evil desires
because they fight against your very souls.* 1 Peter 2:11

✳ D A Y 1

_____

_____

_____

_____

_____

✳ D A Y 2

_____

_____

_____

_____

_____

✳ D A Y 3

_____

_____

_____

_____

_____

✻ D A Y   4

_____

_____

_____

_____

_____

✻ D A Y   5

_____

_____

_____

_____

PRAYER REQUESTS

_____

_____

_____

GOD'S RESPONSE AND MY THOUGHTS

_____

_____

_____

According to our purpose shall be the success of our spiritual progress; and much diligence is necessary to him that will show progress. And if he that firmly purposeth often faileth, what shall he do that seldom purposeth anything, or with little resolution?
Thomas à Kempis

WEEK TWO *Preserve It*

Therefore, since we are surrounded by such a huge crowd of witnesses to the life of faith, let us strip off every weight that slows us down, especially the sin that so easily hinders our progress. And let us run with endurance the race that God has set before us. We do this by keeping our eyes on Jesus, on whom our faith depends from start to finish. He was willing to die a shameful death on the cross because of the joy he knew would be his afterward. Now he is seated in the place of highest honor beside God's throne in heaven. Hebrews 12:1-2

✼ DAY 1

✼ DAY 2

✼ DAY 3

✳ D A Y   4

_____

_____

_____

_____

✳ D A Y   5

_____

_____

_____

_____

PRAYER REQUESTS

_____

_____

GOD'S RESPONSE AND MY THOUGHTS

_____

_____

It is necessary that your foundation consist of more than prayer and contemplation. If you do not strive for the virtues and practice them, you will always be dwarfs. And, please God, it will be only a matter of not growing, for you already know that whoever does not increase decreases. I hold that love, where present, cannot possibly be content with remaining always the same.
St. Teresa of Avila

WEEK THREE *Preserve It*

Work hard so God can approve you. Be a good worker,
one who does not need to be ashamed and who correctly
explains the word of truth. 2 Timothy 2:15

✳ D A Y 1

_____

_____

_____

_____

_____

✳ D A Y 2

_____

_____

_____

_____

_____

✳ D A Y 3

_____

_____

_____

_____

_____

✻ D A Y 4

_____

_____

_____

_____

✻ D A Y 5

_____

_____

_____

_____

PRAYER REQUESTS

_____

_____

_____

GOD'S RESPONSE AND MY THOUGHTS

_____

_____

_____

Simply put, the spiritual disciplines have been a matter of following Christ into his practices. He spent a lot of spiritual time alone, he engaged in service, he prayed, he was silent, he fasted, and so on. Think of spiritual disciplines as following him into his practices—obviously we need them more than he did.
Dallas Willard

The spiritual disciplines include the following:
Silence and solitude ◆ Giving ◆ Fasting
Prayer ◆ Meditation (study) ◆ Submission
Worship ◆ Service ◆ Confession ◆ Forgiving

WEEK FOUR *Preserve It*

But you, dear friends, must continue to build your lives on the foundation of your holy faith. And continue to pray as you are directed by the Holy Spirit. . . . And now, all glory to God, who is able to keep you from stumbling, and who will bring you into his glorious presence innocent of sin and with great joy. Jude 1:20, 24

✳ D A Y   1

_____

_____

_____

_____

_____

✳ D A Y   2

_____

_____

_____

_____

_____

✳ D A Y   3

_____

_____

_____

_____

_____

✻ D A Y 4

_____

_____

_____

_____

✻ D A Y 5

_____

_____

_____

_____

PRAYER REQUESTS

_____

_____

_____

GOD'S RESPONSE AND MY THOUGHTS

_____

_____

_____

> *I arise today*
> *Through God's strength to pilot me;*
> *God's might to uphold me,*
> *God's wisdom to guide me,*
> *God's eye to look before me,*
> *God's ear to hear me,*
> *God's word to speak for me,*
> *God's hand to guard me,*
> *God's way to lie before me,*
> *God's shield to protect me.*
> St. Patrick

MONTH EIGHT
The Challenge of Relationships

Try to live in peace with everyone, and seek to live a clean and holy life, for those who are not holy will not see the Lord.

HEBREWS 12:14

There is nothing more precious than the people who make up the texture of our lives: Parents and children. Loved ones and friends. Teachers and students. Acquaintances and coworkers. Each person we encounter broadens our perspective, adds color to our view of the world, and enlarges our set of experiences.

As Christians, we look at relationships with great reverence. People of faith believe that all things come from God and that the individuals God has placed in our lives are, in a sense, spiritual treasures. Most of us have family members we hold dear, friends we cherish, and others who challenge us, inspire us, and make us stronger.

Nonetheless, relating is never easy. Imperfect people come together to form imperfect relationships, and those relationships sometimes involve anger, broken hearts, misunderstandings, and—too often—estrangement. It doesn't have to be that way. The relationship challenge is to engage rather than to flee. It is to see the irritations from others as gifts for developing our own character. While we must set boundaries that protect us from abuse, we must not guard them so tightly that they eliminate anyone who is not willing to follow our lead, attend to our agenda, or be dedicated to meeting only our needs. Our boundaries must include and allow for the realities of imperfection, irritation, and feelings of inferiority in ourselves and in others. The Seven Keys listed below, when applied to relationships, can provide us with elements that will expand our souls and connect us to our Creator, our loved ones, and ourselves.

- Surrender: We go to God and relinquish to him our feelings, ideas, and opinions about others.
- Acceptance: With God's help, we recognize the areas of difficulty that are making our interaction with others difficult or impossible.
- Confession: We communicate with others our failures and shortcomings as they relate to our relationship difficulties.
- Responsibility: We take full ownership for our part in the problem and work to correct it.
- Forgiveness: We forgive others for what they have done (whether they apologize or not) and seek forgiveness for our own wrongdoing, making amends whenever we can.
- Transformation: With God's help we try to find a way to make our painful experiences valuable to others.
- Preservation: We continue the relationship effort, remaining accountable to others and developing spiritual disciplines and gifts as we strengthen our bond with others.

THE FIRST CHALLENGE WE FACE IN SPIRITUAL RENEWAL AND TRANSFORMA-TION IS THE **CHALLENGE OF RELATION-SHIPS.**

WEEK ONE *The Challenge of Relationships*

Dear friends, since God loved us that much, we surely ought to love each other. No one has ever seen God. But if we love each other, God lives in us, and his love has been brought to full expression through us. . . . If someone says, "I love God," but hates a Christian brother or sister, that person is a liar; for if we don't love people we can see, how can we love God, whom we have not seen? 1 John 4:11-12, 20.

✳ D A Y 1

_____

_____

_____

_____

✳ D A Y 2

_____

_____

_____

✳ D A Y 3

_____

_____

_____

_____

_____

✳ D A Y 4

_____

_____

_____

_____

_____

✳ D A Y 5

_____

_____

_____

_____

_____

PRAYER REQUESTS

_____

_____

_____

GOD'S RESPONSE AND MY THOUGHTS

_____

_____

_____

_We fight one another, and envy arms us against one
another. . . . If everyone strives to unsettle the Body of
Christ, where shall we end up? We are engaged in
making Christ's Body a corpse. . . . We declare ourselves
members of one and the same organism, yet we devour
one another like beasts._
St. John Chrysostom

WEEK TWO *The Challenge of Relationships*

God blesses those who work for peace, for they will be called the children of God. Matthew 5:9

❋ D A Y 1

_____

_____

_____

_____

_____

❋ D A Y 2

_____

_____

_____

_____

_____

❋ D A Y 3

_____

_____

_____

_____

_____

✳ D A Y 4

_____

_____

_____

_____

_____

✳ D A Y 5

_____

_____

_____

_____

_____

PRAYER REQUESTS

_____

_____

_____

GOD'S RESPONSE AND MY THOUGHTS

_____

_____

_____

Where love rules, there is no will to power and where power predominates, there love is lacking. The one is the shadow of the other.
Carl Jung

WEEK THREE *The Challenge of Relationships*

Two people can accomplish more than twice as much as one; they get a better return for their labor. If one person falls, the other can reach out and help. But people who are alone when they fall are in real trouble. And on a cold night, two under the same blanket can gain warmth from each other. But how can one be warm alone? A person standing alone can be attacked and defeated, but two can stand back-to-back and conquer. Three are even better, for a triple-braided cord is not easily broken. Ecclesiastes 4:9-12

✳ D A Y   1

_____

_____

_____

_____

✳ D A Y   2

_____

_____

_____

_____

✳ D A Y   3

_____

_____

_____

_____

_____

✳ D A Y 4

_____

_____

_____

_____

_____

✳ D A Y 5

_____

_____

_____

_____

_____

PRAYER REQUESTS

_____

_____

_____

GOD'S RESPONSE AND MY THOUGHTS

_____

_____

_____

_____

Love is swift, sincere, pious, pleasant, gentle, strong, patient, faithful, prudent, long-suffering, manly and never seeking his own; for wheresoever a man seeketh his own, there he falleth from love.
John Huss

WEEK FOUR *The Challenge of Relationships*

Love is patient and kind. Love is not jealous or boastful or proud or rude. Love does not demand its own way. Love is not irritable, and it keeps no record of when it has been wronged. It is never glad about injustice but rejoices whenever the truth wins out. Love never gives up, never loses faith, is always hopeful, and endures through every circumstance. Love will last forever, but prophecy and speaking in unknown languages and special knowledge will all disappear. 1 Corinthians 13:4-8

✲ DAY 1

✲ DAY 2

✲ DAY 3

✳ D A Y 4

_____

_____

_____

_____

✳ D A Y 5

_____

_____

_____

_____

PRAYER REQUESTS

_____

_____

GOD'S RESPONSE AND MY THOUGHTS

_____

_____

_____

*The Christian ideal has not been tried and found
wanting; it has been found difficult and left untried.*
G. K. Chesterton

MONTH NINE
The Challenge of Obstacles: Fear and Anxiety

He said, "Listen, King Jehoshaphat! Listen, all you people of Judah and Jerusalem! This is what the Lord says: Do not be afraid! Don't be discouraged by this mighty army, for the battle is not yours, but God's."

2 CHRONICLES 20:15

From time to time, we all encounter obstacles to our spiritual health, and among the most frequently experienced obstacles are fear, anxiety, and panic. Feelings of fear are, essentially, a good response to a potentially bad situation, and they are not inappropriate in and of themselves. Like flashing lights along a roadway, they advise us of possible trouble ahead. Without feelings of fear, we would be unprepared when facing physical dangers. But not all fears are the same.

Ongoing or unrealistic fears and anxieties may indicate deeper problems such as unresolved pain, rebellion, willfulness, immorality, or lack of faith. They may exist because we are concerned about the consequences of our behavior or because we feel estranged from God. Whatever the root problems of our fears may be, it is those specific problems that are in need of spiritual renewal and transformation.

Counselors agree that in order to overcome our fears, we must face them. And we can confront our fears and anxieties by applying the Seven Keys to them.

- ◆ Surrender: We examine our fears and release to God the concerns and issues that they represent.
- ◆ Acceptance: With God's help, we face up to the realities that lie behind our fears and accept the fact that they are real and that they are overwhelming us.
- ◆ Confession: We communicate with others the truth about our fears and anxieties, as well as any sins or shortcomings that may be contributing to our fears.

- Responsibility: We own our fears and allow ourselves, with God's help, to face them.
- Forgiveness: We release to God any sin, failure, or weakness that may be causing us to feel guilt, and we forgive others for any pain they may have caused us. We seek peace within ourselves and between ourselves and others by asking their forgiveness if necessary and by making restitution for harm we may have caused.
- Transformation: As we overcome our fears, we seek ways of using our experiences to help others in similar difficulties.
- Preservation: We persevere in our efforts to overcome fear and anxiety, continuing to seek prayer and counsel from others and actively pursuing an ongoing relationship with God.

THE SECOND CHALLENGE WE FACE IN SPIRITUAL RENEWAL AND TRANSFORMATION IS THE **CHALLENGE OF FEARS AND ANXIETIES.**

WEEK ONE *The Challenge of Fears and Anxieties*

Such love has no fear because perfect love expels all fear. If we are afraid, it is for fear of judgment, and this shows that his love has not been perfected in us. We love each other as a result of his loving us first.
1 John 4:18-19

✳ D A Y 1

_____

_____

_____

_____

_____

✳ D A Y 2

_____

_____

_____

_____

✳ D A Y 3

_____

_____

_____

_____

✻ DAY 4

_____
_____
_____
_____
_____

✻ DAY 5

_____
_____
_____
_____
_____

PRAYER REQUESTS

_____
_____
_____

GOD'S RESPONSE AND MY THOUGHTS

_____
_____
_____

Fear not, little flock, from the cross to the throne,
from death into life He went for His own.
Paul Rader

WEEK TWO *The Challenge of Fears and Anxieties*

Can anything ever separate us from Christ's love? Does it mean he no longer loves us if we have trouble or calamity, or are persecuted, or are hungry or cold or in danger or threatened with death? (Even the Scriptures say, "For your sake we are killed every day; we are being slaughtered like sheep.") No, despite all these things, overwhelming victory is ours through Christ, who loved us. And I am convinced that nothing can ever separate us from his love. Death can't, and life can't. The angels can't, and the demons can't. Our fears for today, our worries about tomorrow, and even the powers of hell can't keep God's love away. Whether we are high above the sky or in the deepest ocean, nothing in all creation will ever be able to separate us from the love of God that is revealed in Christ Jesus our Lord. Romans 8:35-39

✻ DAY 1

✻ DAY 2

✲ DAY 3

✲ DAY 4

✲ DAY 5

PRAYER REQUESTS

GOD'S RESPONSE AND MY THOUGHTS

You gain strength, courage and confidence by every experience in which you really stop to look fear in the face. You are able to say to yourself, "I lived through this horror. I can take the next thing that comes along." . . . You must do the thing you think you cannot do.
Eleanor Roosevelt

WEEK THREE *The Challenge of Fears and Anxieties*

But Jesus spoke to them at once. "It's all right," he said. "I am here! Don't be afraid." Then Peter called to him, "Lord, if it's really you, tell me to come to you by walking on water." "All right, come," Jesus said. So Peter went over the side of the boat and walked on the water toward Jesus. But when he looked around at the high waves, he was terrified and began to sink. "Save me, Lord!" he shouted. Instantly Jesus reached out his hand and grabbed him. "You don't have much faith," Jesus said. "Why did you doubt me?" Matthew 14:27-31

✳ D A Y 1

_____

_____

_____

_____

✳ D A Y 2

_____

_____

_____

_____

✳ D A Y 3

_____

_____

_____

_____

✳ D A Y 4

_____

_____

_____

_____

_____

✳ D A Y 5

_____

_____

_____

_____

_____

PRAYER REQUESTS

_____

_____

GOD'S RESPONSE AND MY THOUGHTS

_____

_____

_____

If you are experiencing fear, if you are buffeted by anxiety, if you are seized by sudden attacks of panic, follow Peter's example. Then forget the sea, the storm, the sinking feeling.

Call out to him, exactly the way Peter did: "Save me, Lord!" The Scripture reports, "Instantly Jesus reached out his hand and grabbed him."

Fear not. Be not afraid. He will do the same for you.

WEEK FOUR *The Challenge of Fears and Anxieties*

You will not even need to fight. Take your positions; then stand still and watch the Lord's victory. He is with you, O people. . . . Do not be afraid or discouraged. Go out there tomorrow, for the Lord is with you!
2 Chronicles 20:17

✻ D A Y   1

_____

_____

_____

_____

_____

✻ D A Y   2

_____

_____

_____

_____

_____

✻ D A Y   3

_____

_____

_____

_____

_____

✳ D A Y 4

_____

_____

_____

_____

_____

✳ D A Y 5

_____

_____

_____

_____

_____

PRAYER REQUESTS

_____

_____

_____

GOD'S RESPONSE AND MY THOUGHTS

_____

_____

_____

I dare not fear, since certainly I know
That I am in God's keeping, shielded so
From all that else would harm, and in the hour
Of stern temptation strengthened by His power;
I tread no path in life to Him unknown;
I lift no burden, bear no pain, alone:
My soul a calm, sure hiding-place has found:
The everlasting arms my life surround.
Robert Browning

MONTH
TEN
The Challenge of Downhearted Emotions: Discouragement, Disillusionment, and Depression

And Nehemiah continued, "Go and celebrate with a feast of choice foods and sweet drinks, and share gifts of food with people who have nothing prepared. This is a sacred day before our Lord. Don't be dejected and sad, for the joy of the Lord is your strength!"

NEHEMIAH 8:10

As we seek to know God, we will inevitably pass through shadowed times. For the sake of our growth and purity, we can be sure that God will lead us, from time to time, through emotions that seem incompatible with "the joy of the Lord."

It is for our greater good that we must pass through the darkness. To walk in truth, we must confront our falsehood. To walk in hope, we must confront our despair. To walk in the power of the resurrection, we must confront the Cross—our Lord's cross and our own.

When we are faced with sorrowful feelings—discouragement, disillusionment, depression, or even despair, we can find help as we apply the Seven Keys to our emotional lives.

◆ Surrender: When we are carrying the weight of the world on our shoulders, and that weight is causing us to lose hope, we need to begin the process of renewal by surrendering our world—and its heaviness—to God.
◆ Acceptance: No matter how unhappy we feel, we reject denial, and we face our anger, our hurts, and our fears instead of "stuffing" them. We refuse to carry on with our lives as if nothing were wrong.
◆ Confession: Depression, discouragement, and despair often occur when we turn inward rather than choose to share our burden or private sin with others. Therefore, we communicate with others the truth about our lives.
◆ Responsibility: When we do not own our feelings, we are inclined to repress them. When we do not take responsibility for our lives, we render our-

selves victims. Both of these factors contribute to unhappiness, so we choose to own our feelings and take responsibility for our circumstances.

◆ Forgiveness: Unforgiveness is a major source of depression. We must forgive those who have wronged us, and perhaps most of all, we must forgive ourselves. We must also see the forgiveness of those we have hurt and attempt to make amends in every way we can.

◆ Transformation: As we work with God to redeem our difficult circumstances, we move out from under the shadows of failure, loss, and disability. There is profound joy in knowing that the greatest misery in our lives can be changed into a fulfilling mission.

◆ Preservation: The preservation of our new lives can prevent the return of our spiritual depression. By walking in the light of accountability, spiritual discipline, and thoughtfully invested gifts of the Spirit, we step out of the darkness.

THE THIRD CHALLENGE WE FACE IN SPIRITUAL RENEWAL AND TRANSFORMA-TION IS THE **CHALLENGE OF DISCOURAGE-MENT, DISILLUSION-MENT, AND DEPRESSION.**

WEEK ONE *The Challenge of Downhearted Emotions*

The Lamb who stands in front of the throne will be their Shepherd. He will lead them to the springs of life-giving water. And God will wipe away all their tears.
Revelation 7:17

✻ D A Y   1

_____

_____

_____

_____

_____

✻ D A Y   2

_____

_____

_____

_____

_____

✻ D A Y   3

_____

_____

_____

_____

_____

✳ D A Y 4

_____

_____

_____

_____

_____

✳ D A Y 5

_____

_____

_____

_____

_____

PRAYER REQUESTS

_____

_____

_____

GOD'S RESPONSE AND MY THOUGHTS

_____

_____

_____

To strengthen hope . . .
First, study the Word of God diligently
Secondly, keep a pure conscience
Thirdly, ask God for a stronger hope
Fourthly, increase your love
Fifthly, exercise your hope, and
Sixthly, recall past mercies.
William Gurnall

WEEK TWO *The Challenge of Downhearted Emotions*

Even youths will become exhausted, and young men will give up. But those who wait on the Lord will find new strength. They will fly high on wings like eagles. They will run and not grow weary. They will walk and not faint. Isaiah 40:30-31

✻ D A Y   1

_____

_____

_____

_____

_____

✻ D A Y   2

_____

_____

_____

_____

✻ D A Y   3

_____

_____

_____

_____

_____

✳ D A Y 4

_____

_____

_____

_____

✳ D A Y 5

_____

_____

_____

_____

PRAYER REQUESTS

_____

_____

GOD'S RESPONSE AND MY THOUGHTS

_____

_____

_____

Hope means to keep living amid desperation
and to keep humming in darkness.
Hoping is knowing that there is love;
it is trust in tomorrow, it is falling asleep
and waking again when the sun rises.
In the midst of a gale at sea, it is to discover land.
In the eyes of another it is to see that he understands
*   you.*
As long as there is still hope there will also be prayer.
And God will be holding you
in his hands.
Henri Nouwen

WEEK THREE *The Challenge of Downhearted Emotions*

Because of our faith, Christ has brought us into this place of highest privilege where we now stand, and we confidently and joyfully look forward to sharing God's glory. We can rejoice, too, when we run into problems and trials, for we know that they are good for us—they help us learn to endure. And endurance develops strength of character in us, and character strengthens our confident expectation of salvation. And this expectation will not disappoint us. For we know how dearly God loves us, because he has given us the Holy Spirit to fill our hearts with his love. Romans 5:2-5

✳ D A Y   1

_____

_____

_____

_____

_____

✳ D A Y   2

_____

_____

_____

_____

_____

✳ D A Y 3

_____

_____

_____

_____

✳ D A Y 4

_____

_____

_____

_____

✳ D A Y 5

_____

_____

_____

_____

PRAYER REQUESTS

_____

_____

_____

GOD'S RESPONSE AND MY THOUGHTS

_____

_____

_____

*I pray that God, who gives you hope, will keep you happy
and full of peace as you believe in him. May you over-
flow with hope through the power of the Holy Spirit.*
Romans 15:13

WEEK FOUR *The Challenge of Downhearted Emotions*

Those who trust in the Lord are as secure as Mount Zion; they will not be defeated but will endure forever.
Psalm 125:1

✱ D A Y 1

_____

_____

_____

_____

_____

✱ D A Y 2

_____

_____

_____

_____

_____

✱ D A Y 3

_____

_____

_____

_____

_____

✲ DAY 4

✲ DAY 5

PRAYER REQUESTS

GOD'S RESPONSE AND MY THOUGHTS

My hope is built on nothing less than Jesus' blood and righteousness;
I dare not trust the sweetest frame, but wholly lean on Jesus' name.

When darkness veils His lovely face, I rest on His unchanging grace;
In every high and stormy gale, my anchor holds within the vale.

On Christ, the solid rock, I stand;
All other ground is sinking sand,
All other ground is sinking sand.
Edward Mote

MONTH ELEVEN
The Challenge of Ambitions, Passions, Stressors, and Burnout

Human plans, no matter how wise or well advised, cannot stand against the Lord.

PROVERBS 21:30

What are the primary motivators of our lives? Alongside the drive to make money, we may be competitive creatures who thrive on rivalry and simply want to rise to the top, whatever the top is for us. We may crave power over others and feel insecure unless we are in charge. We may hunger for fame, publicity, and public approval. We may be passionately committed to providing a good life for our family. Or we may genuinely seek to bring the light of Christ into a dark world.

All of these are real drives that inspire real people. They may overlap. And they may occasionally conflict with and contradict each other. Christians often find themselves caught between positive and negative forces as we attempt to fulfill our roles in the workplace. Some of these forces are external, placed upon us by employers, coworkers, and corporate expectations. Others are internal, involving our personal dreams, finances, and values. Even the roles of homemaking and child rearing are not immune to ambitious motives, arrogant attitudes, and self-serving behavior.

We are all fueled by various ambitions and passions, and unless those drives are brought under the control of God, they can become obstacles rather than positive forces. The Seven Keys can be applied to our passions and ambitions, thus alleviating or even preventing stress and burnout.

- ◆ Surrender: We lay all our intentions, desires, and goals before God and relinquish our future to him.
- ◆ Acceptance: We commit ourselves to seeing our lives realistically, and we choose to examine our

conduct to be sure that it reflects Christ's gospel, values, and loving principles. We see our pride, greed, and other negative motivators for what they are.

♦ Confession: We confess to others the sins, short-comings, and weaknesses that are present in our passions and ambitions, and we also share our struggles with stress and burnout.

♦ Responsibility: We take responsibility for our motives, behaviors, and goals, and we allow ourselves to face and feel the fear, shame, pride, or other negative emotions that may be driving us.

♦ Forgiveness: We forgive those who have caused us pain in the area of our passions and ambitions, and we seek the forgiveness of those we have hurt, cheated, or failed, making whatever restitution is possible.

♦ Transformation: With God's help and guidance, we redirect our passions and ambitions in a positive direction, using the lessons we have learned and our experiences with stress and burnout to help others.

♦ Preservation: We choose to allow spiritual disciplines, prayer, and accountability to other believers to monitor our ambitions and passions.

THE FOURTH CHALLENGE WE FACE IN SPIRITUAL RENEWAL AND TRANSFORMA-TION IS THE **CHALLENGE OF AMBITION AND PASSION, STRESS AND BURNOUT.**

WEEK ONE *The Challenge of Ambitions and Passions*

Do not worship any other gods besides me. Exodus 20:3

Dear children, keep away from anything that might take God's place in your hearts. 1 John 5:21

✲ DAY 1

✲ DAY 2

✲ DAY 3

✳ D A Y 4

_____

_____

_____

_____

_____

✳ D A Y 5

_____

_____

_____

_____

_____

PRAYER REQUESTS

_____

_____

_____

GOD'S RESPONSE AND MY THOUGHTS

_____

_____

_____

Any problem, person, or pleasure occupying your waking or sleeping moments which distracts you from your faith, influences your passions, or pulls you away from your Christian community, has in essence been elevated to godlike status in your life. It has become your God.
David Allen

WEEK TWO *The Challenge of Ambitions and Passions*

No one can serve two masters. For you will hate one and love the other, or be devoted to one and despise the other. You cannot serve both God and money. Luke 16:13

✳ D A Y 1

_____

_____

_____

_____

_____

✳ D A Y 2

_____

_____

_____

_____

✳ D A Y 3

_____

_____

_____

_____

_____

✻ D A Y 4

_____

_____

_____

_____

✻ D A Y 5

_____

_____

_____

_____

PRAYER REQUESTS

_____

_____

_____

GOD'S RESPONSE AND MY THOUGHTS

_____

_____

_____

All bow down before wealth.
 Wealth is that to which the multitude of men pay an instinctive homage.
 They measure happiness by wealth; and by wealth they measure respectability. . . .
 It is an homage resulting from a profound faith . . .
 that with wealth he may do all things. . . .
John Henry Cardinal Newman

WEEK THREE *The Challenge of Ambitions and Passions*

But when the Holy Spirit controls our lives, he will produce this kind of fruit in us: love, joy, peace, patience, kindness, goodness, faithfulness, gentleness, and self-control. Here there is no conflict with the law. Those who belong to Christ Jesus have nailed the passions and desires of their sinful nature to his cross and crucified them there. Galatians 5:22-24

✳ D A Y 1

_____

_____

_____

_____

✳ D A Y 2

_____

_____

_____

_____

✳ D A Y 3

_____

_____

_____

_____

_____

✳ D A Y   4

_____
_____
_____
_____

✳ D A Y   5

_____
_____
_____
_____

PRAYER REQUESTS

_____
_____

GOD'S RESPONSE AND MY THOUGHTS

_____
_____

If you need wisdom—if you want to know what God wants you to do—ask him, and he will gladly tell you. He will not resent your asking.
James 1:5

WEEK FOUR *The Challenge of Ambitions and Passions*

Is anyone thirsty? Come and drink—even if you have no money! Come, take your choice of wine or milk—it's all free! Why spend your money on food that does not give you strength? Why pay for food that does you no good? Listen, and I will tell you where to get food that is good for the soul! Isaiah 55:1-2

✻ D A Y   1

_____

_____

_____

_____

✻ D A Y   2

_____

_____

_____

_____

✻ D A Y   3

_____

_____

_____

_____

_____

✳ D A Y 4

_____

_____

_____

_____

_____

✳ D A Y 5

_____

_____

_____

_____

_____

PRAYER REQUESTS

_____

_____

_____

GOD'S RESPONSE AND MY THOUGHTS

_____

_____

_____

The world is too much with us, late and soon,
Getting and spending, we lay waste our powers;
Little we see in Nature that is ours.
We have given our hearts away,
A sordid boon!
William Wordsworth

MONTH TWELVE
The Challenge of Life's Traps: Obsessions, Compulsions, and Addictions

Have mercy on me, O God, because of your unfailing love. Because of your great compassion, blot out the stain of my sins. Wash me clean from my guilt. Purify me from my sin.

PSALM 51:1-2

Why are some people more inclined toward addictive behavior than others? This may have to do with their physical makeup as well as with their past or their emotional needs. But God's solutions are available to all of us. In fact, the weaker we are, the more he is able to be strong in us.

Everyone who is awake and alert to God's presence and holiness struggles with something. Obsessions and compulsions tell us a great deal about ourselves. As we look at them in light of God's wisdom, they help us come to terms with our wounds, they teach us about our fears, and they point out our inability to live independent of God and others.

Obsessions, compulsions, and addictions also remind us that although sin is part of our humanness, Jesus died and rose again to defeat sin and death. His resurrection power—the same power that raised him from the dead—is available to each of us for use in our daily lives. Even if we are not able to overcome our own inadequacies, Jesus is able. There is great strength that comes from saying, "I can't. He can. I'll let him." By applying the Seven Keys to our obsessive, compulsive, and addictive behaviors, we allow him freedom to work in our lives.

- Surrender: Our surrender to God should always include the prayer, "Please reveal to me anything that is coming between you and me."
- Acceptance: We must see our obsessions, compulsions, and addictions for what they are, in spite of the denial that inevitably accompanies them. Acceptance requires us to open our eyes and to

reject our natural tendency to protect our present way of life.

- ◆ Confession: The words are simple and direct: "I am obsessing. I am behaving compulsively. I am addicted. I need to stop, but I can't break the cycle without the help of God. I need your help too."
- ◆ Responsibility: By owning our unhealthy habits, we begin to look at the reasons we developed them. What is the source of the emotional emptiness that triggers our obsessions and compulsions? How did pain thrust us into our addictive cycle? As we own the reality of an unhealthy behavior pattern, we must also own the truth about its sources.
- ◆ Forgiveness: We forgive ourselves for our weaknesses. We forgive those who have hurt us, so that we are no longer carrying around unnecessary pain and bitterness. And, rather than hide behind our sick behaviors, we seek the forgiveness of those we have harmed and make restitution wherever and whenever we can.
- ◆ Transformation: Allowing God to redeem our situation provides us with the opportunity, as the modern aphorism suggests, to "turn our scars into stars." This simply means that we seek to help others in ways that reflect our own spiritual brokenness and renovation.
- ◆ Preservation: By being accountable to others and by practicing spiritual disciplines and gifts, we are able to keep ourselves addiction free, healthy, whole, and transformed by the renewing of our mind.

THE FOURTH CHALLENGE WE FACE IN SPIRITUAL RENEWAL AND TRANSFORMATION IS THE **CHALLENGE OF OBSESSIONS, COMPULSIONS, AND ADDICTIONS.**

WEEK ONE *The Challenge of Addictive Behaviors*

The sacrifice you want is a broken spirit. A broken and repentant heart, O God, you will not despise.
Psalm 51:17

✻ D A Y 1

✻ D A Y 2

✻ D A Y 3

✳ D A Y   4

_____

_____

_____

_____

✳ D A Y   5

_____

_____

_____

_____

PRAYER REQUESTS

_____

_____

_____

GOD'S RESPONSE AND MY THOUGHTS

_____

_____

_____

Is it still a "want" or has it become a "need"?
Do I make my plans to fit around it?
Do I think about it all the time?
Does it distract me from doing my best work?
Has it ever created problems with others?
Has it ever caused me financial problems?
Could it hurt me physically, emotionally, or spiritually?
Is it a secret?
Does it make me feel guilty?
Do I do it more often than I used to?
Do I make and break promises to myself about it?
Does it cause me to compromise my morals or
    values?

WEEK TWO *The Challenge of Addictive Behaviors*

I don't understand myself at all, for I really want to do what is right, but I don't do it. Instead, I do the very thing I hate. Romans 7:15

✳ D A Y 1

_____

_____

_____

_____

_____

✳ D A Y 2

_____

_____

_____

_____

_____

✳ D A Y 3

_____

_____

_____

_____

_____

✳ D A Y 4

_____

_____

_____

_____

_____

✳ D A Y 5

_____

_____

_____

_____

_____

PRAYER REQUESTS

_____

_____

_____

GOD'S RESPONSE AND MY THOUGHTS

_____

_____

_____

_____

Then I said, "My destruction is sealed, for I am a sinful man and a member of a sinful race. Yet I have seen the King, the Lord Almighty!" Then one of the seraphim flew over to the altar, and he picked up a burning coal with a pair of tongs. He touched my lips with it and said, "See, this coal has touched your lips. Now your guilt is removed, and your sins are forgiven."
Isaiah 6:5-7

WEEK THREE *The Challenge of*
Addictive Behaviors

So, dear brothers and sisters, you have no obligation
whatsoever to do what your sinful nature urges you to
do. For if you keep on following it, you will perish. But if
through the power of the Holy Spirit you turn from it
and its evil deeds, you will live. For all who are led by
the Spirit of God are children of God. Romans 8:12-14

✳ D A Y 1

_____

_____

_____

_____

_____

✳ D A Y 2

_____

_____

_____

_____

_____

✳ D A Y 3

_____

_____

_____

_____

_____

✲ DAY 4

✲ DAY 5

PRAYER REQUESTS

GOD'S RESPONSE AND MY THOUGHTS

Some obsessions, compulsions, and addictions hook us into bad things. Others simply cause us to crave too much of a good thing.

Food
Achievement/Success
Religion
Shopping/Spending
Relationships/Spouse
Perfectionism
Music
Computers/Internet
Making/Saving/
 Investing Money
Pet(s)
New Age/Occult Practices
Fitness/Beauty/Appearance
High-Risk Activities
Sex/Romance
Entertainment (Soaps/
 Novels/Films)
Child/Children/Grand-
 children

WEEK FOUR *The Challenge of Addictive Behaviors*

You have patiently suffered for me without quitting. But I have this complaint against you. You don't love me or each other as you did at first! Revelation 2:3-4

✳ D A Y 1

_____

_____

_____

_____

_____

✳ D A Y 2

_____

_____

_____

_____

_____

✳ D A Y 3

_____

_____

_____

_____

_____

✲ DAY 4

✲ DAY 5

PRAYER REQUESTS

GOD'S RESPONSE AND MY THOUGHTS

Recall then that you have received the spiritual seal, the spirit of wisdom and understanding, the spirit of right judgment and courage, the spirit of knowledge and reverence, the spirit of holy fear in God's presence. Guard what you have received. God the Father has marked you with his sign; Christ the Lord has confirmed you and has placed his pledge, the Spirit, in your hearts.
St. Ambrose

Praise,
Thanksgiving,
Honoring
Jesus,
Service

A WEEK OF *Praise*

I will thank you, Lord, in front of all the people. I will sing your praises among the nations. For your unfailing love is higher than the heavens. Your faithfulness reaches to the clouds. Be exalted, O God, above the highest heavens. May your glory shine over all the earth.
Psalm 108:3-5

✻ D A Y 1

_____

_____

_____

_____

✻ D A Y 2

_____

_____

_____

_____

✻ D A Y 3

_____

_____

_____

_____

_____

✲ DAY 4

✲ DAY 5

PRAYER REQUESTS

GOD'S RESPONSE AND MY THOUGHTS

O worship the King, all glorious above,
O gratefully sing His power and His love;
Our Shield and Defender, the Ancient of Days,
Pavilioned in splendor, and girded with praise.

O tell of His might, O sing of His grace,
Whose robe is the light, whose canopy space;
His chariots of wrath the deep thunderclouds form,
And dark is His path on the wings of the storm.

Frail children of dust, and feeble as frail,
In Thee do we trust, nor find Thee to fail;
Thy mercies how tender, how firm to the end,
Our Maker, Defender, Redeemer, and Friend.
Robert Grant

A WEEK OF *Thanksgiving*

Give thanks to the Lord, for he is good! His faithful love endures forever. Give thanks to the God of gods. His faithful love endures forever. Give thanks to the Lord of lords. His faithful love endures forever. . . . Give thanks to the God of heaven. His faithful love endures forever.
Psalm 136:1-3, 26

✲ DAY 1

✲ DAY 2

✲ DAY 3

✻ D A Y 4

_____

_____

_____

_____

_____

✻ D A Y 5

_____

_____

_____

_____

PRAYER REQUESTS

_____

_____

_____

GOD'S RESPONSE AND MY THOUGHTS

_____

_____

_____

> Almighty God, Father of all mercies,
> We your unworthy servants give you humble thanks
> For all Your goodness and loving-kindness to us and to
>   all men.
> We bless You for our creation, preservation,
> and all the blessings of this life;
> But above all for Your incomparable love
> in the redemption of the world by our Lord Jesus Christ;
> for the means of grace,
> and for the hope of glory.
> The Great Thanksgiving, *Book of Common Prayer*

A WEEK OF *Honoring Jesus*

Yes, I am the vine; you are the branches. Those who remain in me, and I in them, will produce much fruit. For apart from me you can do nothing. John 15:5

✳ D A Y   1

✳ D A Y   2

✳ D A Y   3

✳ D A Y 4

_____

_____

_____

✳ D A Y 5

_____

_____

_____

PRAYER REQUESTS

_____

_____

_____

GOD'S RESPONSE AND MY THOUGHTS

_____

_____

_____

Christ be with me, Christ before me, Christ behind me,
Christ in me, Christ beneath me, Christ above me,
Christ on my right, Christ on my left,
Christ when I lie down, Christ when I sit down, Christ
   when I arise,
Christ in the heart of every man who thinks of me,
Christ in the mouth of every one who speaks of me,
Christ in every eye that sees me,
Christ in every ear that hears me.
St. Patrick

Jesus loves me! this I know, for the Bible tells me so.
Anna Bartlett Warner

A WEEK OF *Service*

*Your attitude should be the same that Christ Jesus had.
Though he was God, he did not demand and cling to his
rights as God. He made himself nothing; he took the
humble position of a slave and appeared in human form.
And in human form he obediently humbled himself even
further by dying a criminal's death on a cross.*
Philippians 2:5-8

✳ D A Y   1

_____

_____

_____

_____

_____

✳ D A Y   2

_____

_____

_____

_____

_____

✳ D A Y   3

_____

_____

_____

_____

_____

✳ D A Y 4

_____

_____

_____

_____

_____

✳ D A Y 5

_____

_____

_____

_____

_____

PRAYER REQUESTS

_____

_____

GOD'S RESPONSE AND MY THOUGHTS

_____

_____

_____

Make us worthy, Lord, to serve our fellow men
throughout the world
who live and die in poverty and hunger.
Give them, through our hands, this day their daily bread,
and by our understanding love give Peace and Joy.
Mother Teresa